NATIONAL GEOGRAPHIC

Ladders

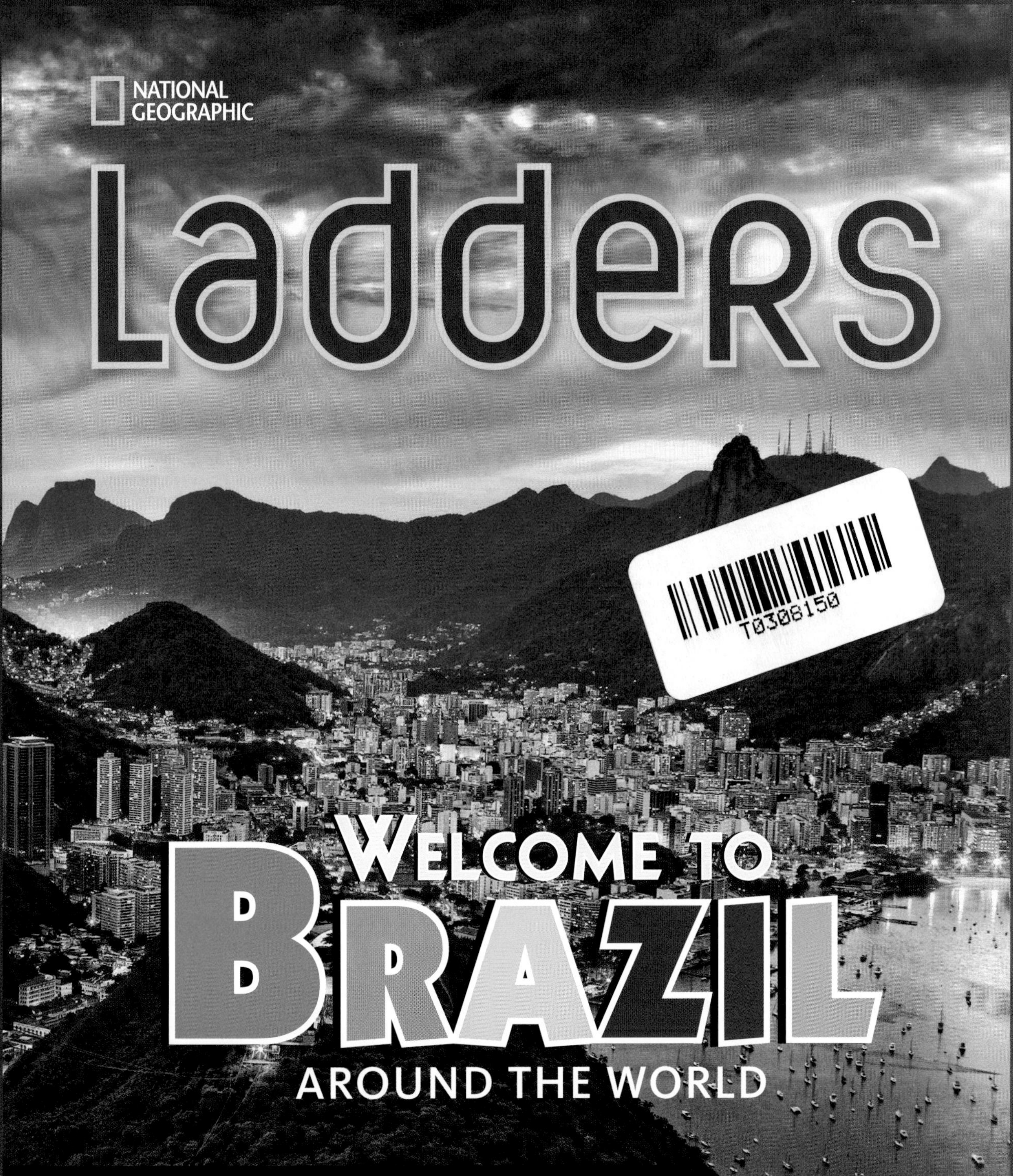

Welcome to Brazil

Around the World

GENRE Social Studies Article **Read to find out** about Brazil's Amazon rain forest.

Into the Rain Forest

by David Holford

Brazil is the largest country in South America. About half of Brazil is covered by the largest **rain forest** on Earth, the Amazon rain forest. Rain forests are warm and wet places with many different kinds of animals, plants, and trees. As you might guess, a rain forest gets quite a bit of rain. If you lived there, you would always need to carry an umbrella because it rains almost every day.

Brazil's rain forest gets its name from the Amazon River. This long river winds between the tall trees of the forest for many miles.

The Amazon rain forest is home to unusual fish, like the electric eel. This fish looks like a snake. Its body can store up electric shocks. When the time is right, it can zap its enemies!

More types of plants and animals make their homes in the Amazon rain forest than any other place in the world. Most of the animals live in the **canopy**. The canopy is a thick layer of tree branches and leaves that covers the top of the forest. It is like a roof. Chattering monkeys, colorful parrots, and lots of other animals spend their entire lives living in the canopy. Many of them never even touch the forest floor.

A Home in the Forest

The Amazon rain forest isn't just full of giant trees and brightly colored animals. Humans live there, too. Many **tribes**, or groups of people that share the same language and beliefs, spend their lives climbing the trees and hunting the animals of the forest. One of these tribes calls themselves the Yanomami (yah-noh-MAH-mee).

The Yanomami live in villages scattered throughout the forest. Several families live together in large, round houses built with vines and leaves. The men and older boys hunt monkeys, birds, and other animals for food with bows and poison arrows.

Besides hunting, the Yanomami grow gardens for food. Both the men and the women work to plant gardens. They chop down trees and plants on small areas of land. Then they carefully set the cuttings on fire. This burning clears parts of the rain forest to make room for a garden.

Once the clearing and burning is done, the women of the village plant and tend the crops. The women's work is hard but important because much of the tribe's food comes from the gardens.

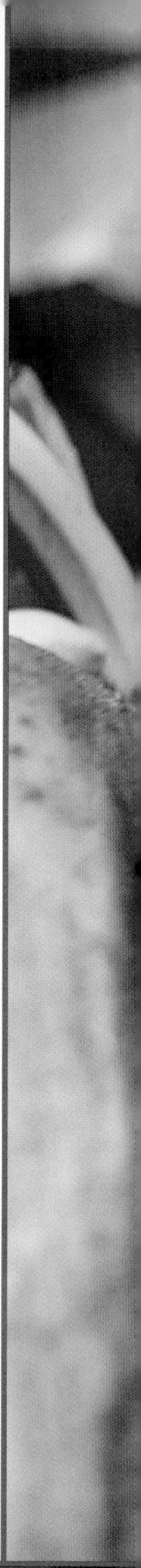

This Yanomami girl wears flowers and paints her face for a celebration.

Instead of a cat or a dog, this young Yanomami man keeps two parrots as pets.

This boy picked these bananas from a tree. The feathers on his head are from a parrot. The Yanomami get everything they need to live from the rain forest.

Squirrel Monkey

Red-and-Green Macaw

Green Anaconda Snake

Three-Toed Sloth

Giant Anteater

Pink River Dolphin

Respect the Rain Forest

The Yanomami respect, or honor, the Amazon rain forest because it gives them the things they must have to live. For example, they use plants and animals for things like food, clothing, and building homes. But the Yanomami take no more than what their families need to stay alive. They know that taking more than what they need would hurt the rain forest and everything that lives there. The Yanomami give back to the forest by treating it well.

Many Brazilians who live outside the rain forest feel the same as the Yanomami. They work hard to protect the rain forest from people who are cutting it down. Cutting down the rain forest destroys the homes of the animals that live there. It also wastes many useful plants that grow there. Some of these plants are even used to make important medicines that save lives.

People on vacation like to visit the Amazon rain forest to see the tall trees and colorful animals. These visitors can help protect the rain forest, too. When they visit, they can be careful to leave no trace of their trip in the forest, just like the Yanomami.

Tiger-Legged Monkey Tree Frog

Check In Why is the Amazon rain forest important to people who live in Brazil and visit the country?

GENRE Culture Article

Read to find out about Carnival in Brazil.

Let's Go to Carnival!

by Hugh Westrup

> During each day of Carnival, more than 2 million people gather in the streets to celebrate. That's one big party!

It's Celebration Time

Imagine the Fourth of July, the Super Bowl, and Halloween all wrapped into one holiday. If you lived in Brazil, you could celebrate something like this each year during **Carnival** (kar-nuh-VAHL). Brazilians call Carnival "the biggest party on the planet."

Carnival is a holiday full of amazing sights and toe-tapping music. For four days, people forget about work and school. They eat their favorite meals. They dress in colorful costumes and walk through the streets. They dance to the music of outdoor bands.

In the Brazilian city of Rio de Janeiro (REE-oh day zhuh-NAIR-roh), the highlight of Carnival is a parade of floats. A float is a decorated platform on wheels that is pulled by a car. You may have seen a float in your hometown parade. Each float is built by one of the city's **Samba** schools. Samba is a style of dance and a type of music. But a Samba school is probably not what you think it is. It's not a place people go to learn. It's a club made up of neighbors. Each Samba school works together to prepare a fun, colorful float for Carnival.

People spend thousands of hours painting a float. They use just as many gallons of paint.

A man makes a big flower for a float. This flower makes up one small part of a huge float.

It's a good thing grasshoppers aren't this big in real life!

Top-Secret Floats

Samba schools work all year to prepare for Carnival. Once Carnival ends, planning for the next year begins right away. Each Samba school develops a **theme**, or big idea, for its float. Everything on the float relates to that theme. For example, the theme might be about a place that is special to Brazil, such as the Amazon rain forest.

Floats are put together inside huge buildings. The floats are very big, so the Samba schools need a lot of room to work. Many people work together to build one float. For example, for a float that shows the Amazon rain forest, carpenters might construct a very large riverboat. Artists might make rain forest animals out of cloth and wire, and flowers out of paper and glue. Everything about the float is kept secret until Carnival. Each Samba school wants its float to be a big surprise to the crowd!

Get Up and Dance!

The heartbeat of Carnival is the Samba, which is music with quick drumbeats and lively horns. When you hear this music, it's impossible not to get up and dance! Each Samba school chooses a new Samba song every year. This is the music the dancers dance to during the parades. Before Carnival, Samba school dancers practice their moves over and over until they are ready to show off to the crowd.

It takes many people to make the costumes for Carnival dancers and musicians. Every outfit is made by hand. For months on end, sewing machines hum inside homes throughout the neighborhood. Six miles of cloth, thousands of feathers, and millions of sparkling decorations called sequins make up the costumes for Carnival each year.

The colors of the costumes are bright—flaming red, canary yellow, shocking pink, peacock blue. But the costumes themselves must be cool and comfortable. Carnival is held in late February or early March, which is the warmest time of the year in Brazil.

These dancers are wearing butterfly costumes. Because they are raised above the other performers, it looks like they are flying.

This woman is called the "Queen of Drums." She leads the drummers in the parade.

Dancers perform in groups called *wings*. Each wing has as many as 100 dancers. Everyone in the wing wears the same costume.

A float makes its way through a cheering crowd in the Sambadrome. Forty judges decide which float is the best.

Parade Time

During the four nights of Carnival, Samba schools show off a year's worth of hard work in a place called the **Sambadrome**. This huge building has no roof. It's like an outdoor stage. A long road stretches down the middle of the building. Bleachers rise up on both sides of the road so the judges and cheering crowds see the floats as they pass by. As each Samba school enters the Sambadrome, the excited crowd claps their hands and cheers.

The last two nights of Carnival feature the 12 best Samba schools. Each school has 80 minutes to perform for the judges and the crowd. First, the Samba school's flag is proudly carried into the Sambadrome. The drummers enter with a thundering wave of sound from their instruments. Then the dancers shake and twirl to the band's music, looking like colorful birds.

Finally, the floats enter the Sambadrome. The crowd goes wild because this is what they have been waiting for. Only one Samba school can win the float contest. But no matter which school wins, the people of Rio de Janeiro have shown off their incredible talents and imagination. They have put on one of the greatest shows on Earth!

Check In How does a community work together during Carnival?

GENRE Folk Tale **Read to find out** about the Brazilian beetle.

How Beetle Got Her Coat

retold by Jenny Loomis

illustrated by Cecilia Rébora

Long ago, cultures from different parts of the world made up stories to explain things they saw in nature. Why does an elephant have a long trunk? Why does a mosquito buzz? Why is the sky blue? These stories often used talking animals to teach lessons about how to behave. In this folk tale from Brazil, we find out how the Brazilian beetle got its colorful coat.

One hot afternoon, Beetle took a stroll through the rain forest. She loved to look at the orchids (AWR-kihdz) after the morning rains had stopped. As she walked slowly along a little dirt path, she admired the brilliant colors of the beautiful flowers. Their velvety petals came in every shade of the rainbow. She particularly liked the shimmery blues and deep lime greens. Beetle looked at her own dull brown coat and sighed, "If only my coat was as colorful as the orchids."

Suddenly, Beetle heard splashing coming from the river, so she turned toward the sound and saw Rat swimming in her direction. He cheerfully jumped out of the water and said, "Poor Beetle! How slowly you walk! It must take you forever to get anything done. It's really too bad that you aren't more like me. I move so fast I'll make your head spin. Watch!"

Beetle just rolled her eyes and continued walking. She found it best to ignore Rat when he started bragging.

Rat did not like to be ignored, so he sped down the path, kicking up chunks of dirt behind him. He did a cartwheel over a rotten tree root to show off, and then he turned around and ran back to Beetle. "HA! That was pretty amazing, don't you agree, Beetle?"

This annoyed Beetle very much. She was just about to tell Rat to bug off when she heard a voice coming from high above the path: "Quite amazing, indeed, Rat."

Startled, both Beetle and Rat looked up to see Parrot grinning and looking down at them from the very top of a banana tree.

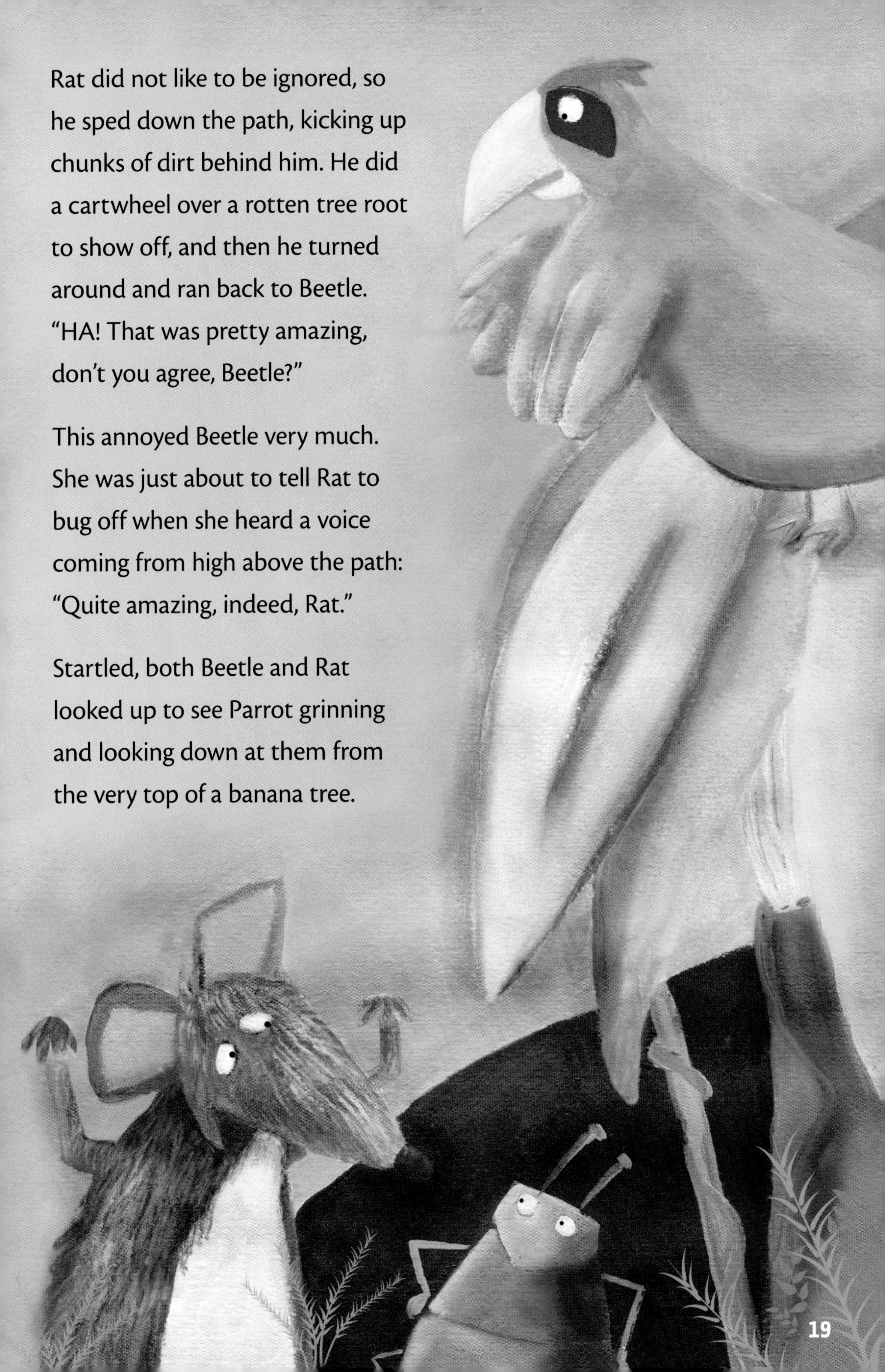

"Your speed gives me an idea for a race. The winner's prize will be a beautiful coat in any color he or she likes. Interested?" asked Parrot.

Rat began jumping with excitement. "Oh, this is great! I'm finally going to have a shiny black coat like Panther! No one notices how fast I am because my brown and white coat is so boring. Once I get a black coat, the other animals will give me the attention I deserve. Let's get this race started," squeaked Rat loudly.

The thought of having a new colorful coat made Beetle happy, so she also agreed to the race.

"Terrific! You'll race to that very large nut tree, and whoever reaches it first is the winner. Ready? GO!" yelled Parrot.

Rat ran as fast as he could without looking behind him. All the while he was dreaming about how handsome he would look in his new black coat. He did a joyful little dance when he arrived at the tree. Looking around for Parrot, Rat announced, "I won, Parrot! I want my shiny black coat now!"

Rat looked up at the nut tree, and couldn't believe what he saw. Sitting next to Parrot was Beetle wearing a sparkling blue and green coat.

"How did you get here so fast, Beetle? I didn't see you pass me," asked Rat angrily.

"I flew up here, of course," replied Beetle.

"Flew? I didn't know you could fly!" yelled Rat.

"Rat, you don't know anything about me. The only time you talk to me is when you're making fun of me," explained Beetle. "You thought I looked slow and helpless, but you were wrong."

Rat angrily kicked the nut tree, shaking a Brazil nut loose. It fell directly on his head.

From that day on, Beetle could be seen in the rain forest, proudly wearing her fancy blue and green coat. She was as colorful as the orchids she admired during her long afternoon walks.

Rat still had his same old coat, but he changed in other ways. He realized he didn't know much about the other animals in the forest. Rat stopped judging them by how they looked—especially the ones he thought he might have to race one day!

Check In Why did Rat think that Beetle could not win the race?

Discuss

1. What connections can you make among the three selections that you read in this book?

2. In what ways do the Yanomami people depend on the Amazon rain forest? What could happen to their way of life if the rain forest is not protected?

3. Tell about the tradition of Carnival in Brazil. Describe how a tradition in your country is similar to Carnival.

4. Folk tales often use animals to teach lessons about how to behave. What lessons did you learn by reading this folk tale?

5. What do you still wonder about life in Brazil?